INDIA
Pre-Historic and Proto-Historic Periods

INDIA
Pre-Historic
and
Proto-Historic Periods

PUBLICATIONS DIVISION
MINISTRY OF INFORMATION AND BROADCASTING
GOVERNMENT OF INDIA

First Edition : February 1981 (*Saka 1902*)
Seventh Reprint : 2021 (*Saka 1942*)

ISBN-978-93-5409-132-2
HIST-ENG-REP-124-2020-21

Price : ₹50.00

Published by:
The Director General, Publications Division,
Ministry of Information and Broadcasting,
Government of India, Soochna Bhawan,
CGO Complex, Lodhi Road, New Delhi-110003

http://www.publicationsdivision.nic.in

Editor : Roma Chatterjee

Cover Design : Rajender Kumar

Sales Centres : • Soochna Bhavan, C.G.O. Complex, Lodhi Road, **New Delhi**-110003 • Hall No. 196, Old Secretariat, **Delhi**-110054 • 701, B-Wing, Kendriya Sadan, Belapur, **Navi Mumbai**-400614 • 8, Esplanade East, **Kolkata**-700069 • 'A' Wing, Rajaji Bhawan, Besant Nagar, **Chennai**-600090 • Press Road, Near Govt. Press, **Thiruvananthapuram**-695001 • Room No. 204. 2nd Floor CGO Towers, Kavadiguda, **Hyderabad**-500080 • 1st Floor, 'F' Wing, Kendriya Sadan, Koramangala, **Bengaluru**-560034 • Bihar State Co-operative Bank Building, Ashoka Rajpath, **Patna**-800004 • Hall No. 1, 2nd Floor, Kendriya Bhawan, Sector-H, Aliganj, **Lucknow**-226024

Typesetter : Quick Prints, Naraina, New Delhi-110 028.

Printed at : Impact Promotions, B-97/1, Naraina Industrial Area, Phase-1,N.D-28

Preface

Sir William Hunter's well-known book *The Indian Empire* was published in 1881. It was revised and published in four volumes in 1907-09 under the title *The Imperial Gazetteer of India.* These four volumes have now been revised and brought up-to-date. They are entitled *The Gazetteer of India: Indian Union.* The second volume—*History and Culture*—was published in 1973.

Some of the chapters of this volume, namely, Government and Economic Life; Society, Religion and Literature; Arts and Architecture; Pre-Historic and Proto-Historic Periods; Early History of India up to A.D. 1206; and History of Medieval India (A.D. 1206—A.D. 1761) which have a wider public opinion, are being published separately in the form of booklets. The idea is to provide to the general public especially the university students, low-priced publications containing authentic and objective information on these subjects by well-known writers who are experts in their respective fields.

Vincent A. Smith contributed the chapter on Pre-historic Antiquities to the *Imperial Gazetteer of India.* There are three contributors to the revised chapter on Pre-historic and Proto-historic periods in the *Gazetteer of India* on which this booklet is based. These are H.D. Sankalia, B.B. Lal and B. Subbarao. It is hoped that not only this booklet but the entire series will have a useful purpose and meet the requirements of the general public.

New Delhi
March 28, 1979

P.N. Chopra
Editor (Gazetteers)

Contents

I
Pre-Historic Period

PRE-HISTORIC AND PROTO-HISTORIC archaeology has been hitherto divided into the Stone Age, Copper Age and Iron Age. Such divisions have stressed only one aspect of man's life over a stretch of nearly 5,00,000 years, namely, the tools and weapons he commonly used. While these suggest the various steps by which man acquired knowledge not only of the two important metals, copper and iron, but also of the manufacture of specialized stone tools and their hafting, they do not, however, adequately indicate man's many-sided ways of life. Knowledge of man's economic and social status and his environment deserves greater emphasis. This objective calls for more data of the dim past than are available today. With the increasing aid from the various scientific disciplines, it is possible to visualize, even if faintly, some of the main milestones on man's march to civilization.

During the long Stone Age, estimated to cover over 5,00,000 years and forming part of the latest geological period, namely, Pleistocene, man was a savage, had no fixed habitation, and could not produce his food, collected plants and fruits, caught fish and hunted wild animals. Changes in environment and circumstances brought about changes in tools. From large, crude and heavy tools there developed smaller, finer, and more specialized ones; a history of man's development based mainly on the study of his tools is therefore possible. And when this is coupled with the flora and fauna deduced from the fossil plants and animals, pollen grains, soils, rise and fall of sea and river levels, solar radiation and several other factors, one gets a more detailed picture of man's life. Such terms as the Stone Age are therefore no longer adequate, the emphasis having shifted from the object to the idea behind it. The stages in man's progress are :

1. Primitive Food Collecting Stage or Early and Middle Stone Ages.
2. Advanced Food Collecting Stage or Late Stone Age / Mesolithic.
3. Transition to Incipient Food Production or Early Neolithic.
4. Settled Village Communities or Advanced Neolithic / Chalcolithic
5. Urbanization or Bronze Age.

Early Stone Age

Since there are marked differences in environment and tool traditions between the Punjab and Peninsular India, it is better to treat them separately. Until 1939, only a part of the Punjab which now falls in Western Pakistan had yielded definite traces of three or four Stone Age Cultures. These have been called Pre-Soan, Early Sohan, Late Sohan and Evolved Sohan, or Chopper-Chopping and Flake-and-B1ade Industries. The first four names are after Sohan or Soān, one of the important tributaries of the Sindhu, along the banks of which the first artifacts were found. The latter group is named after the functional and technological character of the tools and broadly shows man's intellectual as well as material development.

Intensive study began in the foothills of the South-western Himālayas. These constitute the Siwaliks and the Potwar plateau. The latter is a part of ancient Pancanada, drained by the Sindhu, Sohan, Jhelum, Rāvi, Sutlej, and Beas; it includes Rāwalpindi and other districts of Western Punjab. The various geological formations on these rivers were correlated by De Terra and Paterson with the onset and retreat of glaciers during the Pleistocene in the Kashmir valley. This has enabled archaeologists to work out a sequence of climatic fluctuations illustrating the environment of man from the Pleistocene to the Holocene or the present times. When colder conditions (Glacial periods) prevailed in the hills and higher altitudes, the plains of the Punjab were covered with gravels and silts; whereas under warm temperate conditions (interglacial periods) the ice retreated from the hills to higher altitudes and caused erosion in the plains. It is against this fluctuating climatic background that man's activities are to be studied.

Man's presence was believed to have been first noticed in the Boulder Conglomerate which forms the topmost surface in the Sindhu, Sohan and other rivers. During the Second Ice Age in the Kashmir valley, the Potwar plateau experienced very heavy rain and the rivers carried away boulders. This helped to form the Boulder Conglomerate. In this formation were found huge flakes and split pebbles of quartzite. Some of these were regarded as artifacts, as they showed traces of chipping on the side. To distinguish this industry from the later industries, it was called Pre-Sohan, but now it is thought that there are no clear signs of man's work on these flakes and pebbles. We may, therefore, say that man did not exist during the Second Ice Age.

The story then begins with the Sohan Industry. It reveals tools made of split pebbles and flakes of quartzite and greenish grey trap. These have been found at 65 and 125 m. respectively, above the level of the present Sohan and Indus rivers in terrace I (T_1),* formed by the tilting of Boulder Conglomerate and its consequent erosion by the first rivers. This erosion was due partly to the steepening of valley gradients through mountain uplift and partly to increased water supply as a result of the melting of ice. Both in the Kashmir valley and the Punjab plains, genial climate due to interglacial conditions seems to have prevailed. Under such favourable climatic conditions, two distinct types of stone tools have been found : the handaxe and pebble tools, and a few flake tools. The latter are so atypical and, different from fhe former that the industry typified by them is called Chopper-Chopping or Sohan Industry. It is remarkable that both these groups of tools are found in one and the same deposit, but at different places.

When the climate changed, Kashmir was under a mantle of ice for the third time. In the Potwar plateau the streams started fresh erosion, and aggradation, spreading first fine gravel and then silt. Then followed a drier phase during which an intense wind activity began. As a result fine silt called 'loess' was carried over great heights. These deposits formed a second terrace (T_2) in the Sindhu and Sohan valleys.

Man was present at these times and witnessed profound changes on the surface of the land. His tools differ to some extent from those previously found in the Sohan. These occur in the basal Potwar gravel and in the lower 6m. of the silt. But the cores and flakes show some previous preparation and recall not only the 'Levalloisian technique' but also a change in the mode of life, when flakes were preferred for cutting up animals such as horse, bison, camel and wolf, the remains of which occur in the Potwar 'loess'. Any way, stratigraphically, climatically and culturally, there is a distinct change.

---

* Terraces are flat grounds along rivers or lakes or along the sea-shore. These are formed on account of climatic changes which involve rise or fall of the water-level. The higher the terrace, the earlier, it is. Terrace I would thus be older than Terrace 2 and so on.

The entire region once again underwent a change. Interglacial conditions reappeared and a new terrace (T_3) was formed as a result of erosion, but so far no tools of man have been found in the formation. During the Third Interglacial, we have no evidence of change in the late Sohan Industry. But after the Fourth Glaciation, when a new terrace (T_4) was formed on the Sindhu and the Sohan, still finer blade-like tools are found at two localities Pindi Gheb and Dhok Pathan now in Pakistan. This has been designated Evolved Sohan or Upper Palaeolithic Industry.

If such tools had been made in large numbers, they would have heralded a great change in Early Man's life, as they have done in Europe and West Asia. Recent excavations in the Sanghāo cave in the Peshāwar valley (ancient Gandhāra) revealed a flake-and-blade industry, said to be of Moustetian tradition, and placed in the Late Palaeolithic (Middle Stone Age) when the climate was very cold. It is further said that the Middle Stone Age tools in India are probably related to this industry.

The development of the handaxe is not clear. It is said to be of the same antiquity, since it occurs in the deposits of the Second Interglacial period and is believed to have a development parallel to the Sohan Industry till the Third Glacial times, when a developed Handaxe Industry is met with at Chauntra (Pākistān) along with Early and Late Sohan tools.

So, from the outset, two distinct types of tools occur in Western Punjab, at first separately and then together. In the absence of any positive data it is difficult to say whether these imply two distinct human racial types with different modes of life.

In Eastern Punjab, recent explorations around Kangra on the Beas and its tributaries, have also yielded evidence of industries which recall the Early Sohan and Late Sohan. Their exact relationship to the terraces on these rivers and the climatic implications have yet to be worked out.

In the rest of India, not only handaxes but pebble tools, similar to those in the Punjab, have been found from several sites in large numbers. Such a phenomenon would imply that similar conditions might give rise to similar results.

The real home of the Handaxe Culture seems to be according to our present knowledge, Peninsular India, the country south of the Ganga plain. Since the type tools of this culture were first found near Madras, it is also called the Madras Axe Culture; this is a purely regional name which should be given up, as the latest researches, show that the Handaxe Culture covered almost the whole of India—Andhra Pradesh, Madras, Mysore, Maharashtra, Guiarat, Eastern Rajasthan, and the plateau regions of Uttar Pradesh, Bihar and West Bengal—except Western Rajasthan, Sind, Kashmir, Assam and the coastal strips of Andhra, Madras and Kerala. Such a distribution pattern may be due to geographical or ecological reasons, Assam, for instance, is so heavily forested even now that it would have been impossible for the Early Stone Age man to eke out a living. The relics of the Early Stone Age man are mainly confined to the middle reaches of the rivers, and to some distance away from their basins. Altitudes higher than 750 m. and heavily forested regions would also appear to have been avoided by man. No Early Stone Age tools have been found at Mount Abu (Rājasthān), Mahābaleshwar (Mahārāshtra) and the Nilgiris (Madras and Mysore)—ranging from 1,350-2,100 m.

The handaxes and other associated tools first occur in the deposits of the Second Interglacial Age in Western Punjab, whereas in Peninsular India they occur in the earliest pebble conglomerate bed in the Narmadā, which overlies the basal rock or laterite. In this conglomerate are also found remains of such extinct animals as wild elephant, wild horse, wild ox, *Hippopotamus palaeindicus F.* and. C, *Stegodon insignis* F. and C, *Rhinoceros unicomis* Lim, *Sus sp., Trionyx sp., Stegodon ganesa* F. and C, *Emys sp., Ursus namadicus* E. and C., *Leptobos frozen* Rut, *Cervus duvancelli. As* these fauna are placed in Middle Pleistocene, the Handaxe Industry is also ascribed to this period but exactly to which part, it is difficult to say without further data. Recent studies in the Mahi and Narmada basin indicate that this period could not be later than early Upper Pleistocene.

Elsewhere in India also the Handaxe Industry or Culture is generally considered to belong to the Middle Pleistocene. But this should not be taken to mean that Early Man appoared simultaneously all over Peninsular India.

The Early Stone Age tools in the Peninsula include, besides the various forms of handaxes, cleavers, choppers and chopping tool made out of pebbles or pebble-halves and scrapers, some with a regular, well-made place to facilitate holding, picks and a few two-ended, and beaked tools which could have been used for engraving or cutting only. The last mentioned tools occur in the Kṛṣṇā basin in Karṇāṭaka (Northern Mysore).

The handaxe was an all-purpose tool, which assumed various forms. That is true also of cleavers, which could have been used for cutting wood and chopping meat. In both, there are clear instances of a "waist" on either lateral side showing that the tools were hafted in a wood or bamboo stick and secured with a cord and some mastic.

So far, nowhere in India anything but single or groups (some amazingly large) of tools have been found. These are but assemblages which give some insight into the art and industry of their makers, but throw very little light on man and his culture as a whole. The reason, of course, is that so far man's relics namely tools have been found in secondary deposits and his likely habitation sites have to be searched. It is still customary to call these assemblages Handaxe Culture. We are still in the dark about the racial type or types of the makers of these tools who roamed practically all over India, and whether they knew fire as in China or had temporary camps as in East Africa where they had big as well as small game. Except in very few cases, the association of the tools and contemporary animals is not proved, so that we can only tentatively say that certain animals whose remains have been found mostly in the Narmadā and Godāvari valleys were hunted by man. These animals, however, suggest the environment in which man lived—comparatively thick forest, as we find around Hoshangabad and other places in Madhya Pradesh in which teak, banyan, *pipal, palās (Butea Frondosa)* grew in abundance. In the early stages, rain was probably heavier than today and rivers flowed in very broad beds carrying huge pebbles and even boulders. But gradually rain decreased and almost all over India rivers began to shed their load in their beds. These rose to several metres and became cemented with lime solutions from calcareous silt which later covered these deposits.

This is but a faint picture of Early Man and his environment in the Indo-Pākistān subcontinent. In the absence of precise data, except for the two major geographical divisions (the Himālayan foot-hills which were often affected by peri-glacial conditions and Peninsular India which seems to have experienced heavier rainfall) in the middle Pleistocene with their distinct tool traditions, nothing definite can be said about various regions— their climate, flora and fauna.

Middle Stone Age

While further development of the Sohan Industry has beets found in the Punjab, until recently nothing definite could be said about the fate of man in Peninsular India.

Cores and flakes showing previous preparation occur in the deposits— basal Potwar gravel and silt—of the Third Glacial Age. These as welt as the blade-flakes found in the deposits of the Fourth Glacial Age may be provisionally placed in the Middle Stone Age and assigned to the Late Pleistocene. Handaxes have been found in Kangra valley in 1966-67. They belong to the lowest terrace, probably quite late in the Pleistocene. In Peninsular India, deposits containing similar handiwork of man are found resting on or against the older river deposits consisting of pebbly gravel conglomerate and silt. These were laid down like the previous ones during another cycle of wet and dry conditions. The younger deposits are rarely pebbly and coarse and generally finer and more sandy. The tools found in the deposits are as a rule, made of fine-grained material such as flint, jasper, agate and chalcedony, though in some areas like Kurnool and Madras quartzite also was employed. They are comparatively small. A normal assemblage consists of several kinds of scrapers, points, awls or borers, small choppers and chopping tools. All these are generally made out of flakes or flake-like nodules which are flat on one or both sides. In some regions, such as Western Rājasthān and Madhya Pradesh, on the rivers Lūni and Betwa and its tributaries, there is a distinct improvement in the technique of making flakes. This is what is known as "the prepared core" or "faceted platform" technique, reminiscent of the famous Levallois method in France.

Unlike the earlier tools, the small tools are retouched along the edge which is at times fine. Since all over India such assemblages of tools are found in deposits assigned to the Middle Stone Age, it is conceivable that these tools were employed for fashioning larger tools and weapons such as spokeshaves, arrows, lances, and bows of wood, none of which has survived, being of perishable nature.

The nature of the tools as well as the deposits in which these occur suggest a lightly wooded environment where rain was not very heavy and certainly less in intensity and duration than in the Early Stone Age. Man lived along the foot-hills where raw material in the form of veins of chert, agate and flint was easily available. Some of the older mammalian fauna such as the *Bos namadicus* and *Elephas antiquus* seem to have survived, at least in Marlarashtra where their remains have been found in direct association with Middle Stone Age tools. In the absence of skeletal remains, it is difficult to say whether the same race of man continued to inhabit India during this period. Though he was still a hunter-fisher and a savage, a change was indicated in man's *modus operandi by* his toolkit and the materials of which it was made.

Late Stone Age

Though almost all over India and Pākistān the Middle Stone Age industries are followed by still smaller tools {microliths), there is nowhere a clear stratigraphical succession corresponding to a typological evolution. In a large number of cases, the microliths are found on the surface, in sandy or barren rocky surroundings. The latter undoubtedly show that great climatic changes had taken place, but whether these changes should be related to the period when man lived in the area and manufactured these tiny tools or to a later period has not been ascertained in all cases.

The microliths, themselves insignificant, presage a great technological development—the introduction of compound tool. Instead of keeping the stone tools in his hand, man now hafted them in a bone, wooden or Bamboo handle or shaft, and thus were born the prototypes of several kinds of later copper and iron sickles, arrows, harpoons and drills. This device had its origin in the Middle Stone Age, but reached its culmination in this period. Now the tools were universally very small, sometimes barely an inch or a half inch long, and so could not be used otherwise. The pressure technique by which these microliths were made was probably known earlier. Economically man was still a savage, a hunter-fisher. However, in some areas as elsewhere in the world there appeared the next great step—pottery-making with its concomitant of permanent habitation and food production.

In Eastern India, microliths generally occur on the surface of laterite plains and forests in Orissa, Bengal and Chota Nāgpur plateau, and on rocky (sandstone) hillocks in Mirzāpur. The few, small-scale excavations in these regions indicate their probable antiquity and the prevailing climatic conditions. Until recently all these areas were lightly forested. Large Sal trees still dominate the dark-red laterite plateaus and plains in West Bengal and Chota Nagpur plateau. In Mirzāpur, there is a scrub forest in the northern parts, while in the south there are kilometres of rice fields on the edge of low sandstone ranges, which in the past were well-forested.

Excavations at Birbhānpur near Durgāpur railway station on the bank of the Dāmodar river in Burdwān district (West Bengal) show that at first the climate was very wet so that laterite was formed and a dense forest covered the region. A drier phase then followed, and at that time microlith-using mart appeared on the scene. He probably lived in circular huts, the walls of which, to judge from the existence of a few round postholes, were supported by round wooden posts. The tools were generally made of milky quartz, though crystal, chert, chalcedony, quartzite and fossil wood (of which large chunks have been found all over the place) were occasionally used. Typologically, the microliths are non-geometric; that is, such forms as the triangle and trapeze are absent. No pottery is found associated with the microliths. Hence, it is thought that man in this region was still a hunter-fisher and had not taken to incipient cultivation. Since the microlithic habitation layer is covered with two-thirds metre of sandy, light brown earth, one can assign fairly great antiquity to this Late Stone Culture.

The Kaimur range, at the junction of Madhya Pradesh. and Uttar Pradesh, continues the story begun at Birbhānpur. These sandstone formations had provided an ideal shelter as temporary or permanent camps for men of different periods, the earliest of which seems to go back to the advanced food-gathering stage. Small-scale excavations of open air sites and rock-shelters at Morahānā Pahār and Bhaghaikhor near Bhainsaur and at Lekhania, 65 km. from Mirzāpur, yielded first non-geometric microliths and later geometric ones with an ill-baked ochre-red pottery. At Bhaghaikhor, only one skeleton was found. But at Lekhania, the occurrence of about 14 human skeletons in a deposit not more than 42 cm. in thickness suggests that owing to some calamity all these were buried in the same habitation ; or that this was the preferred burial area in the rock-shelter— whenever a person died, he or she was buried there.

The orientation of the body was west-east and in all cases it was laid in an extended fashion.

Later, a people, who buried the dead in large stone-lined pits and covered them with still larger slabs, sometimes only one, and deserve the name megalithic, occupied the area. They used first copper and later iron and also pottery. Thus, a gradual development is witnessed in this region though the details arc not yet available.

The Vindhyan sandstone formations which extend westwards into Madhya Pradesh have also a large number of caves and rock-shelters, many of which were inhabited. Very few unfortunately have been systematically excavated. Excavations at Ādamgarh, near Hoshangābād, brought to light a layer containing palaeoliths at the bottom, and microliths both geometric and non-geometric, associated with a pottery, were found in the uppermost layer of black or brown soil, A few specimens of chalcolithic pottery were found on the surface. Here too, the microliths seem to antedate the chalcolithic phase and appear at a much later date than the Early Stone Age. However, their association with pottery, domesticated animals and rock-shelters undoubtedly shows settled life.

A parallel development also took place in Orissa ; at Kuchaiburi, near Baripāda (former Mayūrbhanj state), microliths were noticed below a layer yielding pottery and ground stone tools.

In the extreme south of India, in the Tirunelveli district, microliths again occur in a context which suggests fairly good antiquity but a dry climate, The coastal area to the south and north of the river Tāmraparni is strewn with fossil sand-dunes locally called *teris.* These were formed when the sea level was higher than what it is today. This was due to a dry climatic phase. Man lived on the *teris* and made microliths of chert, silicified wood and limpid quartz, material which is not available in the region. The industry includes both geometric and non-geometric elements and it is probable that the latter belongs to an older phase of the *teris.*

Slightly better data is available in Central and Northern Gujarāt, where first Lānghnaj and then Akhaj in the Sābarmati basin, and Amrapur in the Mahi basin give us unmistakable association of microliths with an ill-baked pottery, debris of animal bones, and human beings buried within them.

Langhnaj and Akhaj are not solitary sites, but representative of the hundreds which dot the sandy alluvial plains of Northern and Central Gujarāt. The topography is quite different from what one sees in Eastern and Southern India. Out of kilometres of flat, sandy stretches suddenly turn up three or four hillocks of the same material. These enclose an inundation lake, which retains water for almost ten months in a year. The tops and slopes of these hillocks covered with brushwood are strewn with microliths. These as well as the river banks were, therefore, the resorts of microlith people.

Thus the dune surfaces were fixed and small inundation lakes formed by alternating dry and damp phases. The microliths appeared long after the Early Stone Age, but did not find the raw material at hand. Nodules of chert, and quartz and quartzite and chlorite schist which they occasionally used for heavy tools had to be imported from some distance. Microliths include blades (retouched and simple), lunates, trapezes, triangles, scrapers and points and a few burins. The occurrence of one ring-stone or mace-head of quartzite among heavy tools and two small ground or polished tools of chlorite schist seems to be significant. The latter—two small ground tools—seem to be symbolic only, though implying contact with or a knowledge of such tool-making centres. The former suggests either that man had begun to cultivate with the help of a digging stick for which the quartzite ring was used as a weight or that the ring was used as a mace-head.—a powerful offensive weapon. The numerous fragments of small saddle querns of sandstone were evidently meant for preparing a paste with haematite ruddle stones, and not for grinding grain. Pottery, though extremely few, arid ill-fired, is associated with microliths, This suggests that the Stone Age man in Gujarat had at least temporary camps or habitations, of which unfortunately no traces seem to have survived. But there is no evidence that he had taken to producing his own food by incipient cultivation. No animals would seem to have been domesticated, for among the masses of large and small animal remains, occur at least three species of deer—the spotted deer, hog deer, swamp deer—nilgai, the black buck and one-horned rhinoceros, but no sheep or goat.

The presence of rhinoceros implies that the environment provided by lakes and surrounding areas of scrub forests was congenial enough for such animals to flourish, or that the rhinoceros lived on the river banks, where they were hunted by men, and their carcasses brought up to the mound. Fishing also provided food, as the occurrence of pieces of carapace of tortoise and fish vertebrae show.

The dead were buried in a highly crouched posture, preferably in north-south direction, though there are instances of other orientations as well. No definite idea of the race to which the Stone Age man belonged can be formed, since a study of the 13 or 14 skeletons shows traits which are not only characteristic of the Mediterranid and the Veddoid, but also of other racial groups.

The age of this culture is not yet determined. Towards the top, from one metre upwards, occur a ring-stone, small and polished axes of chlorite schist, a large copper knife, an iron arrow-head, and wheel-made pottery, the latter quite different from that found in the early deposits. This sequence definitely indicates a succession of momentous cultural changes in Northern Gujarāt since this stone-using man first appeared on the scene.

In short, the *teris* of South India, Birbhānpur and pre-pottery, non-geometric levels in Mirzāpur in Eastern India, represent early phases of the Late Stone Age. The later phases at Mirzapur and other sites in Uttar Pradesh and Madhya Pradesh and Lānghnaj in Northern Gujarāt, where pottery also occurs without any definite evidence of domestication of animals and incipient agriculture, might represent the next stage.

Elsewhere, in Madhya Pradesh, Eastern and Western Rājasthān, Saurāshtra, Mahārāshtra, Andhra Pradesh and Mysore the finds, so far, have come from surface only. Even here, mictoliths seem to precede the blade tools of the later chalcolithic period. So we may postulate a Late Stone Age in many parts of India, during which the climate was generally dry (with regional variations and corresponding vegetational environment) and. man had not taken to agriculture and domestication of animals.

A very fine blade and burin industry has been found near Renigunta in the Chittoor district, Andhra Pradesh. A microlithic industry was found above a patinated basalt flake industry and below the Neolithic industry at Sangan kalla, Bellary district.* This definitely proves that even in this part of India, the microliths have great antiquity, and indicate a real transition between the pure food-collecting stage and the foodproducing stage.

---

* Excavations at Sangan kalla, Mysore, have yielded evidence to show that in this region, microliths are of considerable antiquity; positively before the Neolithic or Polished Axe Culture or the beginning of agriculture. Since the microlithic deposit underlies the Neolithic and overlies that of an earlier Stone Age industry, it is truly Mesolithic, as in Western Europe. Further, its association with a sticky black brown soil indicates climatic conditions when much more rain fell in the region, which is semi-arid today.

Thus, a real transition between the pure food-collecting stage and the food-producing stage can now be postulated in serveral parts of India.

II
Proto-Historic Period

A CLEAR DEVELOPMENTAL history of the succeeding stages is not yet available from any one area. The picture has to be reconstructed or pieced together from scenes here and there.

The thread of the story interrupted at Lānghnaj may be picked up in Baluchistan. This is a transitional zone lying between the higher inland plateau of Central Asia and the low flat plains of Sind. Not only was the Quetta valley extensively inhabited in pre-historic times, but at a site like Kill Ghul Mohammed near Quetta, a cultural development is found. Here four occapational periods have been identified. During the earliest period dating back to about the middle of the 4th millennium B.C., the people lived in mud-brick houses, used chert and bone tools and domesticated sheep or goat. Some kind of crop production also existed. In the next period, a basket-impressed, hand-made ware came into use. In the third, however, we see two distinctive elements which seem to form, along with the above-mentioned chert tools, the diagnostic traits of the succeeding cultures for quite a iong time. They were wheel-turned, painted pottery, and copper which, with the addition of tin, was not long after hardened into bronze.

The Pre-Harappan Culture of the North-West

There were other chalcolithic villages distinguished from each other mainly on the basis of pottery, and sometimes also supported by other artifacts like terracottas and tools. Encompassing the Baluchi hills were four principal culture-groups : Zhob, Quetta, Nāl and Kulli.

Named, so because of its association mainly with the Zhob valley, but extending southwards into the Loralai district as well, the Zhob Culture is characterized by a red ware painted over in black pigment, now and then supplemented by red and terracotta female figurines with a grim goblinlike face. Also in use were blades, points and leaf shaped arrow-heads of flint, and needles of bone; the use of copper is proved by the occurrence of a rod and a ring at one of the sites (Periano Ghundai). Houses were made of mud-bricks set on boulder-foundations. There is also evidence of fortification at one of these sites (Moghul Ghimdai). Cremation of the dead is indicated at some of the Zhob sites.

The Quetta Culture is distinguished by a buff ware painted over in black pigment, mostly with geometric designs including 'stepped' motifs. Amongst other aspects of this culture are chert blades, bone points, saddle querns, alabaster cups and clay figurines.

South Baluchistan shows two noteworthy cultures, named after their type-sites, Nāl and Kulli respectively. Of these, the former is characterized by a buff ware, usually white-slipped, with attractive polychrome paintings, the basic black or sepia being supplemented by red, green, yellow and blue. Houses were built of stone rubble or mud-brick of both. Flat axes, elongated bar-celts, saws and spearheads of copper were used and fractional burial practised. Associated with the culture were also beads of semi-precious stones, a copper stamp-seal and a perforated stone weight.

Typical of the Kuili Culture is a pinkish-buff ware painted over in black pigment, occasionally augmented by red, with designs of an elongated humped bull, its rounded eyes set within a horizontal panel of landscape. The terracotta female figurines depicted only down to the waist have a pinched face (profile), hold their arms akimbo and are heavily decorated. The animal figurines, mainly the bull, have black stripes. Houses were built usually of stone, though mud-brick was also occasionally used. Other objects associated with the Kulli Culture were chert blades, saddle querns and mullers of stone, and compartmented pots of chlorite schist, the exterior decorated with incised designs. The Kullians cremated, their dead—a practice in marked contrast to that followed by the Nal people or the Harappans.

Proto-Harappan Cultures in Sind, the Punjab and Rajasthan

Traces of culture or cultures preceding the Harappan had been obtained first at Atari, and then at Harappa itself. But it is only now, during the last 10 years, that something definite can be said about these cultures which we may call 'Proto-Harappan', because in some respects they are really ancestral to the Harappan, The earliest of these seems to be the Amri Culture. It was first discovered by the late N.G, Majumdar in 1929 in Sind. Amri is situated one mile west of the Indus, in Dadu district,

300 miles north of Karāchi. Later excavated by Jean Casal (1959-62), these excavations have revealed four Phases in the Amri Culture numbered 1A, IB, 1C and ID. Except burial jars at two levels, very few traces of houses remained in Phase IA*. The pottery is largely handmade, with seven kinds of designs and graffitis on a few of them. But the few wheelmade bowl and rimless pots have thin walls and a pale cream coloured fabric. There is a scrap of copper, many chert blades, stone balls and few terracotta beads and bangles of shell and terracotta. In Phase IB, appear mud-brick houses, and the pottery shows a few changes, the most important being a dish-on-stand and a few bone points. During Phase 1C, the entire mound was occupied and four structural levels are visible on Mound A** and three on Mound B. The houses are rectangular, though of various sizes with doors and mud-floors. The pottery improves in technique and decoration, 55% being wheel-made. In Phase ID occurs a large house with partition, and pottery shows further improvement with biochrome element. Animals are represented for the first time and these as well as other features indicate contact with Baluchistān and Afghānistān. The Harappans arrived at Amri in Period II,

Kot Diji, situated 15 miles south of the Khaipur Division has given a slightly different picture.

It has revealed traces of a defensive wall and well-aligned streets and houses with large communal fire-places and highly sophisticated, wheelmade pottery along with tools and weapons of stone, some of copper and bronze, artistic toys, some very artistic, and cakes and balls. Thus, with the exception of writing and long stone blades, the Kot Dijians had everything that Harappans are known for. There was planning and organization as well as skill of the artist and craftsman.

There is plenty of evidence to show that this proto-Harappan civilization at Kot Diji, which existed according to one Carbon-14***

---

* Usually when habitational Phases / Periods are assigned lables like A, B, C, etc., A is the earliest. Periods are bigger cultural divisions numbered 1, II, III, etc.

** Moulds A and B are parts of the same site. These have been named differently because of the present configuration of the area, which shows these off separately.

*** This is a method of dating the past, and is based on the fact that Carbon-14, a radioactive form of carbon, is being continuously produced in the atmosphere and absorbed by all living organisms.

determination in 2471 ± 141 B.C. was destroyed by fire, possibly caused by the Harappans who were there by 1970 ± 134 B.C.

One more important thing at Kot Diji is that the foundations of the fortification wall and houses are of stone, probably because stone is very easily available, the medieval fort standing on a rock.

Proto-Harappan settlements were not confined to Sind and the Punjab only. They are found in Northern Rājasthān (former Bikaner state) also and possibly extended further west-wards into the Gaṇgā plain. A large number of sites have been discovered, of which Sothi and Kāli Banga are well known. The pottery from Sothi in the ancient Dṛṣadvati valley discovered by Shri A. Ghosh was so distinctive that he designated it as representative of Sothi Culture. Now we call it pre or proto-Harappan from the evidence at Kāli Banga (also called Kāli Banga-I).

Kāli Banga is situated on the ancient Sarasvati, now called Ghaggar. Since the Harappan city overlies the earlier Proto-Harappan, clear house plans of the earlier city are not available. But in some houses, we have evidence of ovens and the well-aligned lane between a row of houses. There is also evidence of mud-brick fortification exposed on the southern, western, and northern sides of Kāli Banga.

It is interesting that like Amri and Kot Diji Kāli Banga should also yield stone blades which are not only small but made on agate and chalcedony; some are serrated and baked.

Copper was known, as it is attested by copper-bead as well as a celt and few other objects. The existence of wheel conveyance is proved by a cart-wheel having a single hub. The pottery has six fabrics, all wheelmade, as at Kot Diji, but unlike Amri, where in the lowest levels, the majority was hand-made. Of the six Carbon-14 determinations available so far, only one TF-155 dates it to 2245 ± 115 B.C., others are later by 75, 100 or even 200 years,

It has been observed by the excavators that the pottery fabrics and forms found at Amri and Kāli Banga show a close affinity with the early Baluchistān and Irānian pottery. Other objects show a similar genetic affinity to the Chalcolithic Cultures of the area, but are different from and inferior to the corresponding Harappan objects, though the author of the excavations at Kot Diji thinks that they are superior.

Amri pottery is quite distinctive. In fact, it was this feature which enabled the first discoverer, over 40 years ago, to postulate the existence of a separate, pre-Harappan Culture. In brief, the fabric is comparatively thin and not so well made as in the Harappan, and in early phases, largely handmade. The bowls are rimless and other vessels have a very low neck. Externally, the surface is pale red or creamy and bears painting in black—commonly a black band round the neck—and occasionally also in red. The painted designs include pot hooks or crooks, horizontal bands with solid triangles sigmas, sun design, and later animals. Intentional rustication or roughening of the lower surface is also a special feature of the Amri and other pre-Harappan pottery.

Though not Carbon-dated, on comparative grounds, the Amri Culture is placed before 2,500 B.C.

Pottery from Kot Diji shows many similar features, though it is all wheel-made. The fabric is thin, the ground colour varying from red to pinkish. This is decorated by fugitive bands, red, sepia, or black round the neck of globular pots as well as bcwls and dishes.

These as well as other features, for instance, a grey ware with dish-on-stand, bowl and basins, appear in the pre-Harappan at Kāli Banga, which has, as mentioned above, six distinct fabrics.

Many more sites have been reported and it appears that this proto-Harappan or pre-Harappan Culture extended far into the Gaṇgā valley, where it was destroyed by a gigantic flood with the result that everywhere— Rūpar, Hastināpur, Atranji-kherā and other sites, the pottery is rolled and was, therefore, described as ochre-coloured pottery. But the recent examination of the pottery from Atranji-kherā showed that it was similar to or identical with the pottery at Sothi having a blacks-band at the neck, and some pottery having beautifully incised decoration. Since there is evidence of town-planning and fortification and good pottery from all the three excavated sites, it is evident that the beginning of civilization was reached by the forerunners of the Harappans. However, the Harappans succeeded in building up an empire and in effacing all smaller regional cultures, because they alone, of all these cultures, could seize the flint quarries of Sukkur and Rohri. The long blade tools and weapons made from this material were far more efficient than the compound tools made by their predecessors. However, this was a slow process, Even co-existence, for instance at Kot Diji, was not ruled out. And it is believed that the Harappan occupation in the region was in fact shorter than the pre/proto-Harappan.

The Indus Civilization (Urbanization)

In marked contrast to the localized village-cultures is the Indus Civilization, also known as the Harappa Civilization or Harappa Culture after the site in the Punjab where it was first identified. Explorations in progress are likely to throw fresh light on the full extent of this civilization; but even as we know it, the area covered by the civilization was much more than that covered by the contemporary civilizations in the Nile or Tigris Euphrates valleys in the west or the Yellow River valley in the east. From Sutkagendor in Southern Baluchistan to Ālamgirpur in the Meerut district of Uttar Pradesh, the known western and eastern limits of the Indus Civilization, it is a distance of over 1,550 km. From north to south, it extends over 1,100 km. between Rūpar in Punjab and Bhagatrāv in the Kim esturary in Gujarāt.

Although it flourished over a vast area, the Indus Civilization presents little variation. Whether it is Harappa or Mohenjodaro, Kali Banga or Lothal, the most striking character is systematic town-planning; the streets oriented north-south and east-west, produced a grid-pattern. Flanking the streets and similarly oriented lanes and by-lanes were well-planned houses, which in the case of Harappa and Mohenjodaro were almost invariably made of kiln-burnt bricks. Elsewhere in the contemporary world, mud-bricks and wattle-and-daub were the usual building materials, and burnt-bricks were altogether unknown.

A house comprised a central courtyard, three to four living rooms, a bath and a kitchen, while the more elaborate ones contained even up to thirty rooms and were often two-storeyed. Many of the houses were provided with a well; and there was an excellent underground drainage system.

Town-planning went further. At Harappa, Mohenjodaro and Kali Banga, there are two blocks of mounds—the large one on the east and a smaller one on the west. While the large block was the 'lower' city with its houses and streets laid out in the manner described above, the other seems to have been a citadel enclosed by a thick (13 metres at Harappa) mud-brick wall, externally revetted with burnt bricks, corner towers, and occasional bastions built along the length. The fortifications at Kali Banga are being studied. Although no separate fortified mound has been found at Lothal, the conception of an acropolis seems to have existed, as may be inferred from the presence of a huge platform over which are situated the more important and large structures.

At Mohenjodaro, there lay in the citadel a 'college', a multi-pillared 'Assembly Hall', a public bath (the Great Bath) and a large granary consisting of a podium of square blocks of burnt-bricks with a wooden superstructure. Such blocks in mud-brick have also been found on the citadel-mound at Kāli Banga and on the acropolis at Lothal, At Harappa, the interior of the citadel has not been adequately excavated. But in the shadow of the citadel has been found a granary consisting of twelve oblong blocks in an area of over 800 sq. m., as at Mohenjodaro. At Harappa, between the granary and the citadel, have also been found a series of circular platforms, probably for the pounding of grain, and two rows of workmen's quarters.

The commodious houses, knit into a system of rigid town-planning, the public buildings, large granaries and the citadel, all combine to present the picture of a prosperous people, controlled by a firm yet beneficent authority.

The extensive use of burnt-bricks, for the firing of which plenty of wood was needed, and the frequent depiction of jungle fauna like the tiger, rhinoceros and bison on the Indus seals suggest that in those days there was perhaps more rainfall in the area than today. Today at Mahenjodaro even 10 cm. of rainfall a year is rare, Besides, the rivers, which have shifted their courses slightly away, seem to have skirted the towns: the Indus, Rāvi, Ghaggar, Sutlej and Bhogāvar (Limrikobhogāwo) skirted Mohenjodaro, Harappa, Kāli Banga, Rūpar and Lothal respectively. Adequate water supply and rich alluvial soil favoured agriculture. There were bumper crops of wheat and barley, besides peas, melons and bananas. There was cultivation of cotton for textiles—a crop unknown in those times even in Egypt. To the dietary were added fish, fowl, mutton, beef and pork. Besides the cattle, both humped and humpless, cats, dogs and probably elephants were domesticated. The evidence regarding horse and camel is inconclusive. On a potsherd from Harappa is found a person wearing a *dhoti,* shawl as an upper garment is suggested by the wellknown steatite statuette from Mohenjodaro, supposed to be of a priest. The occurrence of needles and buttons proves that at least some items of dress might have been stitched.

Life seems to have been gay and happy as shown by the various ways in which the womenfolk dressed their hair and bedecked themselves with necklaces, bracelets, finger-rings, ear-rings, girdles, and anklets. There were diversions, such as dice or hunting wild animals. The young played with marbles, rattles and toys. The bull with a mobile head, and the monkey going up and down a string, show ingenuity.

The terracotta figurines, animal as well as human, and the black-on-red pottery rich with designs, show that even the common man had a taste for the beautiful though his buildings seem to have been drab. The progress which the Indus people had made in the plastic arts is borne out by the two sandstone statuettes from Harappa in which human anatomy is depicted. These figures could well have been the envy of the Greeks, renowned for their sculptural art, two thousand years later. Metal sculpture too was far advanced as shown by the pose and facial expression of the bronze statuette from Mohenjodaro. The seal-cutter's art seems to have reached its zenith. The Brahmani Bull, with, its swinging dewlap, pronounced hump and muscular body, bears a standing testimony to the skill of the Indus craftsman.

From the inscriptions on the seals, pottery and other objects, it is clear that the Indus people knew reading and writing, while the use of weights (in a binary system) and measures (as shown by a scale found at Lothal) proves that they knew arithmetic as well. The script has not been deciphered so far, but overlaps of letters on some of the potsherds from Kāli Banga show that writing was *boustrophedon* or from right to left and from left to right in alternate lines.

The Indus people lived in full-fledged Bronze Age, although chert blades continued to supplement the tool-repertoire. Bronze objects for domestic use included knife-blades, saws, sickles, chisels, fish-hooks, pins, tweezers, mirrors, and a variety of pots. Spears, axes, arrow-heads and short swords might have been used either in self defence against wild animals or in warfare. For the warfare, however, one would have expected better weapons.

While copper might have been obtained from Khetri in Rājasthān and gold from Kolār, lapis lazuli, jade and turquoise seem to have come from Badakhshan, the Pamirs and Khorasan respectively. Imports could have been matched by exports as revealed by bales of cloth from Umma in Mesopotamia bearing the imprint of an Indus seal, The find of seals of Indus style at Ur, Lagash, Susa, Tell Asmar and other places suggests that perhaps some Indian traders were living in Mesopotamia. That this trade was at least partly sea-borne is proved by the discovery of an ancient dockyard at Lothal, connected through the Bhogāvar river with the Gulf of Cambay. One can visualize Indian ships, depicted on a seal and a potsherd from Mohenjodaro, cruising up and down the Arabian sea.

But who were the prime authors of this mighty civilization cannot yet be said with certainty. The skeletal remains in the burials show that the population comprised Mediterraneans, Alpines, Proto-Australoids and Mongoloids.* This cosmopolitan character is reflected in the several religious practices. Some worshipped the Mother Goddess, so popular in

* After a critical appraisal of the changing concepts in physical anthropology and the nature of the skeletal material from excavations at Harappa, Mohenjo-daro, Chanhu-daro and Lothal, all the four important sites of the Harappan Civilization in Punjab, Sind and Gujarat, Dr. D. K. Sen rejects the old view as outmoded and says that at the most we may say that "the Harappans were long-headed and high-domed groups, the sexes not differing markedly in these charecteristics. They had medium high faces and orbits of medium dimensions." The population was markedly broad-nosed as a whole, and reasonably homogeneous.

The sample size from Mohenjo-daro is so small as to be useless for broad-based conclusions, However, long-headedness and fairly good height is indicated in the males, and medium noses in females.

The Lothal sample, all male, exhibits broad-headedness, broad noses and a fairly tall group.

Broadly, at each of these sites the population was homogeneous, with regard to head-shape, nose-shape, and stature. Whatever their original composition, the populations at these sites belonged each to a single biological group and not recognizable as belonging to several races with distinctive characteristics. This population was broad-nosed or chamaerrhine, tall and long-headed in the Punjab and Sind with somewhat rounder heads in Gujarat.

It is, therefore, inferred that the population in India during the Harappan times descended from earlier populations in the same region, and perhaps the Harappan Culture or Civilization is autochthonous.

contemporary West Asia. On some seals is found a horned, three-faced figure surrounded by animals and believed to be the prototype of Siva in the form of Paśupati. There are also several objects identified as *lingas* and *yonis* and fire-places with central stole, found recently at Kāli Banga. Trees, animals, streams and spirits also seem to have been worshipped.

That there was a belief in 'the other world' is shown by the fact that with the dead were interred a large number of pots and toilet objects such as mirror, antimony rod and mother-of pearl. The body was usually placed with the head to the north and lay supine and extended. One at Harappa was found wrapped in a reed shroud and placed in a wooden coffin. Since this was uncommon in the Indus Civilization but usual in contemporary Mesopotamia, it is probable that there lay buried a man from the west. Until recently the main evidence for fixing the date of the Indus Civilization was the seals found in West Asia in levels ascribable to the reign of Satgon of Akkad i.e., around 2300 B.C. On the assumption that the period of large scale trade contacts was also the heyday of the Indus Civilization, its date was fixed at c 2500-1500 B.C. Recent Carbon-14 determinations, however, indicate a shorter duration, namely, c 2400 to 1700 B.C.

The end of the Indus cities is still obscure. The discovery in the upper levels of Mohenjodaro of human skeletons lying pell-mell, with a skull having a cut-mark, points to invasion and massacre, but this interpretation has been rightly challenged. It may be noted that the Cemetery H Culture, found at Harappa and at two sites in the former Bahawalpur state has been associated with invaders. This H Culture, represented by jerry-built walls, black-on-bright-red pottery and two successive burial strata (the lower and upper characterized respectively by complete inhumations and fractional pot-interments) had a clear stratigraphic break from the Harappa Culture itself, signifying a time interval.

Another theory ascribes the end of Mohenjodaro to heavy flooding, for some traces of recent alluvium have been, noticed on hillocks in the lower Indus basin. Traces of flood-havoc have been noted at Lothal also. The excavations in progress at Kali Banga, however, have not so far yielded any evidence either of invaders or of floods, nor are there traces of a general decline such as have been found at Mohenjodaro itself. Here perhaps the drying up of the Ghaggar, owing either to climatic fluctuations or to a diversion of the waters, might have led to the desertion of many sites.

It may be surmised that while individual cities may have been deserted on local or regional considerations, the civilization as a whole did not meet with a sudden and violent end. The devolution of Harappa Culture at Lothal and the Punjab lends support to this view.

The Post-Harappan Cultures of Sind and Baluchistan

A few words may be added on the proto-historic cultures that followed the Harappa Civilization in the Indus valley and Baluchistan. Besides the Cemetery H Culture, already referred to, there are in the Indus valley two important post-Harappa Cultures, named after their type-sites Jhukar and Jhangar respectively. At Chanhu-daro, both these cultures occur in succession above the Harappa Culture. The Jhukar Culture is distinguished by a buff or cream-coloured pottery with designs executed in a purplish-black pigment, often augmented by red. Among other associated objects mention may be made of a bronze shaft-hole axe, pins with decorated heads, also of bronze or copper, and 'compartmented' seals of faience and pottery. Most of these have parallels in West Asia.

The Jhangar ware is grey or greyish-black. It bears incised patterns which include chevrons and hatched triangles. No other trait of the culture is known; nor has it been possible to date it precisely.

In Baluchistan, there are two-principal proto-historic cultures of the post-Harappan times, besides some stray tools of bronze which also seem to have cultural significance. One of these cultures is represented by a cemetery at Shahi Tump, dug into the ruins of a Kulti Culture mound. The burials were complete inhumations, the body lying on one side with flexed legs. Comprising the grave articles were, besides pots of grey, to yellowish-buff ware painted over in black or reddish-brown pigments, a spearhead, a shaft-hole axe and compartmented seals, all of copper and suggesting, as already stated above West Asian affinities.

Another culture is that represented by the burial-cairns at Moghal Ghundai, Jiwanri, Zangian and elsewhere. Associated with it are, besides a red ware, horse-bells, rings, bangles and a tripod jar of bronze or copper, which, again, have parallels in West Asia.

Lastly, then is a bronze sword from Fort Munro and a trunnion celt from Shalozān, the former recalling prototypes from Talish in Caucasia and Luristan in Persia while the latter has several parallels not only in West Asia but also in Europe.

Most of these post-Harappan cultures of Sind and Baluchistān point to lively contacts with West Asia, if not to an actual influx of people.

The Upper Ganga Basin

The story of the Upper Gaṅgā basin is somewhat different from that of the Sindhu. Here the earliest proto-historic culture seems to be that represented by 'Copper Hoards'. They comprise, besides ordinary, shouldered and bar-like celts, hooked spearheads, antennae swords, harpoons with a hook or hole for hafting, rings and 'anthropomorphic' figures, the exact use of the last named is not clear. The more noteworthy sites in the basin yielding this class of tools include Bahādarābad, Rājpur Pārsu, Bisauli, Fatehgarh, Sarthauli, Bithūr, Pariar and Sheorajpur. However, the tools, individually or in groups, have been found even outside this region for example, at Pondi Kalan and Gungeria in Madhya Pradesh, Hami and Baragunda in South Bihar, Tamajuri in the hilly part of West Bengal, Dunria and Bhagrapir in Orissa, Kallūr in Mysore and even at Lothal in Gujarat, if the fragmentary specimen found at the site is a part of an 'anthropomorphic' figure. Although it does not comprise the more characteristic types like the harpoon or the 'anthropomorphic' figure, a hoard from Khurdi in Rajasthan has also been taken by certain scholars to belong to this class. The Copper Hoard Culture in the basin had contacts as far south as Andhra Pradesh. Most of the objects have been secured from dealers or in chance diggings. It is, therefore, not yet possible to say with certainty what ceramic industry went with them. At Bahādarābad, however, there is some reliable circumstantial evidence. Here engineers working on an irrigation project found beneath a 2-3 m. sterile deposit of clay and sand a large number of tools belonging to this category; and archaeologists, following the clue obtained from the same context a red ware, occasionally with greyish core resulting from indifferent firing. Although most of the specimens do not show any slip and their surface rubs off easily leaving an ochrous substance on the finger, there do occur slip-patches on a few sherds. For want of a more suitable name, the ware has provisionally been labelled 'Ochre Colour Ware'. Prior to the digging at Bahādarābād, the Ochre Colour Ware had been obtained in explorations at Rājpur Pārsu and Bisauli, at spots from which the Hoards had been recovered earlier. This suggests a cultural association between the Ware and the Hoards.

At Hastinapur, Meerut district, Uttar Pradesh, sherds of this Ware were found below the Painted Grey Ware, with a clear break in between. This gives to the Ochre Colour Ware a date prior to *c.* 1200 B.C. If the Lothal fragment is what it is surmised to be, the Copper Hoard Culture should be deemed to have coexisted at east with a late stage of the Indus Civilization; probably as its variant.

At Rūpar in the Punjab and at Ālamgirpur in Uttar Pradesh, the Painted Grev Ware Culture found to overlie the Harappa Culture, with a break in between. It may broadly be placed between c 1100 and 600 B.C. The upper limit of this bracket seems to be confirmed by a Carbon-14 determination (1025-110 B.C.) of a charcoal sample from Atranji-khera, district Etah.

The Painted Grey Ware, as the name indicates, is grey in colour and is painted in black pigment. The commoner types are bowls and dishes. The painted designs include simple bands, groups of vertical, oblique and criss-cross lines, sigmas, *swastikas,* chains of short spirals, rows of dots and dashes, concentric circles and semi-circles.

The main concentration of the Painted Grey Ware seems to have been in Southern Punjab, Northern Rājasthān and Western Uttar Pradesh. There are, besides, examples at Lākhiyo Pir in Sind/ Ujjayini in Madhya Pradesh, Sohāgaura in Eastern Uttar Pradesh and Charan in the Punjab. Among the more important sites in the region of concentration, mention may be made of Ahicchatra, Ālamgirpur, Atranji-khera, Bāghpat, Bairāt, Barnāwa, Hastināpur, Indraprastha (Purāna Qila at Delhi), Kuruksetra (Kurukṣhetra), Mathura, Pānipat, Rupar, Srāvasti and Tilpat.

Available evidence shows that the Painted Grey Ware people lived in houses of mud or wattle-and-daub. There is not evidence of kiln-burnt brick; and even that of mud-brick is not very satisfactory. Agriculture and cattle-breeding seem to have been the main, occupation of the people. At Hastinapur, there is evidence of rice, impressions of which occur at Lothal in pottery and in charred remains at Nāvḍāṭoji. To the dietary were also added mutton, beef and pork, as suggested by the occurrence of charred bones with sharp cut-marks of sheep, goat, cattle, buffalo and pig. As for other domesticated animals, particular mention may be made of the horse *(Equus caballus),* the presence of which in the Indus Culture is somewhat doubtful.

The Painted Grey Ware people belonged to a full-fledged metal age—there is no evidence of any lithic tools like microliths or polished stone axes. At Hastinapur have been found an arrow-head, nail-parer and an antimony rod of copper; and although the earlier digging had yielded only slags of iron from the upper strata, subsequent (1962) work has brought to light a few iron artifacts as well. At Ālamgirpur and Atranjikherā, iron objects have been reported to occur right from the beginning of the Painted Grey Ware occupation. They comprise barbed arrowheads, spearheads, nails, etc. Ālamgirpur has also yielded a few terracotta animal figurines with incised decoration and an oblong die of bone. From Hastināpur come bangles of bone and glass, a whetstone of slate and cylindrical objects of chert and jasper. On the basis of evidence from other sites, the last mentioned ones would seem to be ear-studs, probably with a covering of gold foil. Pointed tools of bone might have been used either as arrow-heads or for weaving. They have often been called *styli,* but so far no inscription has been found in the Painted Grey Ware levels.

The Painted Grey Ware occupation at Hastināpur came to an end because of a heavy flood in the Gaṅgā, which washed away a considerable portion of the settlement. Signs of this devastation are left on the mound in the form of an erosional scar, while some of the washed-away material has also been encountered in the river bed at a depth of about 12 m. below the sub-soil water level.

The story of Hastināpur seems to have been continued at Kauśāmbi, further down the valley. Here occur massive mud defences externally revetted, with burnt-bricks, as also a stone-built palace. A first century inscription found in a monastery area at Kausambi identifies the spot as Ghoṣitārāma where the Buddha is known to have stayed during his visit to king Udayana's capital.

Rajasthan

Rajasthan comprises two major geographical units, marked off from each other by the Arāvalli range running south-west to north-east. The north-western region may further be divided into the northerly area comprising the now dry valley of the Ghaggar, and the southerly part consisting of the Thar Desert relieved in the southernmost sector by the Lūni river. The Arāvalli is a classic example of the saying: 'rivers unite and mountains divide.'

In the Ghaggar valley, the pre-Harappan Chalcolithic Culture at Kāli Banga is the earliest proto-historic culture. Whether it had any relationship with the rnicrolithic industries in the same valley, is a matter for further investigation. It is yet to be ascertained how far this pre-Harappan Culture contributed to texture of Harappa Culture. Of the latter, quite a few sites have been explored along the valley, amongst which, in addition to Kāli Banga, Tarkhanwala-Pera may be noted for its size.

The next cultural phase in the Ghaggar valley is represented by the Painted Grey Ware, the more noteworthy sites being Chak-86 and Sardārgarh. An interesting point here is that the Painted Grey Ware people were fond of 'breaking new ground', in contrast at Rūpar or Ālamgirpur they settled on deserted Harappan mounds.

The proto-history of the Thar Desert is not known. In the hilly tracts of South-eastern Rājasthān; the Banās is the principal river. On its banks, as also on those of some of its tributaries, has been discovered a protohistoric culture characterized in the main by a black-and-red ware painted in a pinkish white pigment with linear and pseudo-geometric patterns. Important sites of this culture are Ahar and Gilund, on the outskirts of Udaipur and in the Bhilwāra district respectively. The culture is known after Ahar, the site where it was first identified and also, after the principal river, the Banās.

At Ahar, two main periods have been identified. They belong respectively to the proto-historic Ahar Culture and to early historical times. On the basis of pottery, the former period is further divisible into three sub-periods, IA, IB, and IC. While the characteristic white-painted black-and-red ware continued throughout the period, sub-period IA was distinguished by the presence of buff and cream-slipped wares, the latter disappearing in IB, when a highly-fired, chocolate-coloured ware came into existence. In IC, the bowl in the white-painted black-and-red ware showed distinctive carination, and there also occurred a few sherds of the lustrous red ware typical of the post-Harappa Culture at Rangpur in Gujarāt. It is, therefore, clear that in its last stages the Ahar Culture outlived the Harappa Culture. Carbon-14 determination places the middle levels of sub-period 1A in 1725±140 B.C.

The inhabitants of Ahar lived in large houses made of stone-rubble or wattle-and-daub, with occasional use of mud-bricks. One room is 9 x 4.5 m. At Ground, however, the houses are mostly of mud-bricks and there is also a structure of kiln-burnt bricks. Mention may be made of a series of parallel mud-brick walls, the intermediary space stuffed with sand; it is likely that they represent the podium of a granary; the super structure being that of wood. Hearths, single or composite (the latter having as many as five units), and clay-lined storage pits have also been found. The use of copper is proved by the discovery at Ahar of five celts, besides bangles and rings. The absence of stone tools suggests that the Ahar Culture is of the Copper Age. Other objects associated with the Banās Culture are saddle querns, mullets of stone, animal figurines, gamesmen and spindle whorls of terracotta, many of them with incised patterns.

Central India

By the beginning of the second millennium B.C., parts of Central India, in particular the valleys of the Narmadā and Chambal, had entered the food-producing stage. Where exactly it began is not yet known. Excavations at a few sites—Maheshwar and Nāvḍaṭoḷi on the Narmadā, Āwra and Nāgda on the Chambal and Eran on the Bina—have revealed the existence of people among whose lithic blade tools may still be found a small percentage of microliths. They were farmers, living in settlements with mud-wall fortifications as at Eran, or open and nucleated villages as at Nāvḍaṭoḷi. The houses at the latter site consisted of one or two rooms made by closely set wooden posts. These were further enclosed by a bamboo screen, plastered with clay from inside and outside and coated with lime. The roofs were presumably flat or conical depending upon the plan of the hut, and made with reeds and mud laid on a bamboo screen. There were vessels for cooking, eating, drinking and storing and querns for grinding grain, and several types of mullets for pounding. Small, round, ball-like, stones might have served as sling stones, and others with a flatter base as weights. Except a few small and large storage vessels and huge plates for kneading dough, the pottery is painted. The black-on-red pottery predominates, but there is a small proportion of white-on-cream or yellow and white-on-black surface. The last two occur in Phases I and II, but the former continues throughout the life of the settlement, which on several Carbon-14 determinations lasted for at least 500 years (1700 B.C.– 1200 B.C.). Some of the pottery shapes—the stemmed cups, channel-spouted bowls and small water vessels *(loṭās)*— become rare later and have a graceful outline and design. Nearly 500 of these have been listed. There were two kinds of *cūlhā,* single-mouthed and multi-mouthed, the latter having surprisingly low walls and lime-plastered foreground.

The early farmers grew two kinds, of wheat, a small variety with blunted ends and a longer one with pointed ends. There were five kinds of legumes —*masūr* or lentil, *urd* or black gram, *muṅg* or green gram, *matar* or green peas and *lathyms (rawan),* besides four other unidentified leguminous seeds. Food was probably cooked with linseed oil, as is done even today in parts of Uttar Pradesh. Rice enters the dietary of the inhabitants in Phase II (c.500 B.C.). This is the earliest occurrence of rice as well as lentil, linseed and *urd.*

How these grains were cultivated is not known, for no remains of plough have been found, A large number of stone rings, if not used as mace-heads, might have served as weights for digging sticks.

The stalks of wheat were cut probably with sickles of wood set with chalcedony teeth; likewise knives for cutting and slashing were made with similar small blades of identical stone, thousands of which have been found at Nāvḍaṭoḷi.

While vegetarian food formed the principal part of the diet, the presence of the remains of cattle, pig, sheep or goat in the house debris shows that animals were domesticated and also eaten, at least by a part of the population.

The early farmers of Mālva were apparently fairly well off and perhaps quite selt-sufficient, though probably dependent for copper which was used sparingly and occurs in small quantities as flat axes, fish-hooks, pins, rings and daggers or swords with raised mid-rib. Contact with Rājasthān, Saurāshtra and the Deccan is indicated by the presence of a black-and-red ware painted in white, lustrous red ware and a fine matt-ware respectively.

Whatever be the final date for the disappearance ol this Chalcolithic Culture in Malwa and elsewhere—Eran, Nāgda, Āwra and Maheshwar—it was succeeded by a culture characterized by a plain black-and-red ware, a few sherds of the Northern Black Polished Ware, punch-marked coins and iron. Probably this iron Age was ushered in by the rise of Ujjayini, which according to tradition and literary evidence, was the capital of Pradyota, a contemporary of the Buddha. Like Kauśāmbi, Ujjayini was one of the *Mahājanapadas* of the North and had formidable defences. The fact that it had iron in its earliest phase is confirmed by archaeology.

Eastern India

Eastern India fails into three geographical units: the sub-Himālayan region of Assam, the alluvial plains of the Gaṇgā, and the Chota Nāgpur plateau merging with the hilly tracts of Orissa.

Except for small polished stone axes, the sub-Himalayan region of Assam is *terra incognita* as regards pre-Mstoric and proto-histoiic periods.

At Kuchai in the Mayūrbhanj district of Orissa, the spade has revealed a Neolithic Culture, overlying but separated from the non-geometric microlithic industry of the Birbhānpur type. This culture is characterized by polished stone axes having usually a rectangular or trapezoidatal cross-section, as opposed to the oval cross-section of their southern counterparts. As no specimen of the highly polished shouldered adze with a South East Asian bias has been encountered, it is difficult to say if and where this type fits into the complex; it could have appeared on the scene at a late stage. Found along with the axes at Kuchai was a coarse, brownish-red ware, occasionally slipped and incised. There is at present no evidence to date this culture precisely but *c.* 1000 B.C. may not be far wrong.

The more noteworty findspots of the Copper Hoard Culture are Hami and Baragunda in Bihār, Tamajuri in West Bengal, and Bhagrapir and Dunria in Orissa. Although the 'bar' and 'shouldered' celts are represented in both stone and metal, there is no stratigraphic evidence to determine the relationship between the Copper Hoard and the Eastern Neolithic Cultures.

Unrelated to either of the cultures is the one found in the lower levels of Pāṇḍurājār-ḍhibi, in Burdwan district, West Bengal, It is characterized by white-painted black-and-red and black-on-red wares which, though not the same as their counterparts at Ahar and Navdatoli, may not be altogether unrelated to them. And the difference is perhaps accounted for by the time factor, for Carbon-14 determination places the Pandurajar-ḍhibi Culture in the last quarter of the second millennium B.C. The people lived in houses of wattle-and-daub and used copper tools, rings and bangles. Evidence regarding microliths is doubtful. The occurrence of a few small-sized polished stone axes testifies to their use, though in a limited degree. Fully extended inhumations as well as fractional pot-burials were in vogue,

The Pāṅḍurājār-ḍhibi evidence indicates that a culture, probably a synthesis of Ahar and Central Indian Chalcolithic Cultures, spread eastwards across the Central Indian and Chota Nāgpur plateaus, along the radiating river-systems. The same pattern of culture-movements may explain the presence of a white-painted black-and-red ware in the middle Gaṅgā-valley, for example at Pṛahlāḍpur in Vārānasi district, at Chirand in Saran district, Bihar, and at Sohagaura, in Gorakhpur district Uttar Pradesh. It is not unlikely that the unpainted black-and-red ware occurring in the earliest levels at Sonpur in Southern Bihār may also be the relics of such a diffusion.

At Sonpur, the black-and-red ware is followed by the Northern Black Polished Ware and iron, and a few specimens of polished stone axes which may be stray survivals. The Northern Black Polished Ware phase brings us to the middle of the first millennium B.C. when Vaiśāli and Rājgir, both in Bihār, vied with each other as capitals of the respective kingdoms. A more or less contemporary site in West Bengal seems to have been Tamluk on the mouth of the Rūpnārāyan river, which, at the beginning of the Christian era, became the foremost Indo-Roman trading station in Eastern India.

Gujarat

It is not known what happened to the Lānghnaj people. However, the next phase in Gujarāt seems to be that represented by the Harappa Culture found at Rangpur, Lothal, and Rojdi.

The Harappa Culture in this region has certain peculiarities—white-painted black-and-red ware; it has therefore been termed as 'Saurāshtra' or 'Kāthiāwar Harappan Culture. Contemporary with the Harappan, was a culture identified at Somnāth and a few other coastal sites, and distinguished by bowls of greyish-buff ware with linear and geometric designs on the exterior in a chocolate-to-reddish pigment.

A change in the Harappa Culture at Lothal had set in at the beginning of the 19th century B.C. Harappan painted designs decreased and new pottery. forms came into being. Chert blades were replaced by those of chalcedony and jasper. This was continued at Rangpur where towards the end of Period II, a lustrous red slip began to be applied to the pottery. In Period III, this Lustrous Red Ware became the most dominant ceramic industry. With the Harappans disappeared their town-planning and kiln-burnt bricks.

The Lustrous Red Ware phase was followed by that of plain black-and-red ware, associated with iron. Not long after, the Northern Black Polished Ware also appeared, bringing the story well into early historical times.

Northern Deccan

After crossing the Narmadā, one comes across two twins of chalcolithic sites: Prakāsha and Korat on the northern and southern banks of the Tāpti respectively, and Bahāl and Tekvāda located on the banks of the Girna, a tributary of the Tapti, In each case, the first site represents a settlement and the other a burial-ground.

Further south, in the upper Godāvari valley, a somewhat different culture-complex seems to have been evolved. At Daimabād, Ahmadnagar district, the occupational strata falls into three sub-periods. In sub-period A, the inhabitants used microliths, polished stone axes and a coarse grey ware with incised and applique decorations, there also being a few black-on-red sherds. The black-on-red ware, however, became dominant in the following sub-period—some of the painted designs were similar to those from Prakāsha and Nāvḍāṭoji. There was also, a piece of the channel-spouted bowl in the Mālwa ware, leaving little doubt about trans-Narmada contacts. But during this sub-period also occur a few examples of the tubular spout which, together with the carination at the waist of bowls, became the distinctive feature ol the pottery in sub-period C. The ware with these typical shapes and a matt, red surface, has been found at many other sites in the Deccan, including Jorwe, .Nevāsa and Chāṇdoli.

The Jorwe or Northern Deccan. Chalcolithic people lived in houses of mud or wattle-and-daub and used, besides the above-mentioned pottery, blades, points, borers and scrapers of jasper and chalcedony, polished axes of fine-grained basalt, celts, rings, and bangles of copper and beads of semi-precious stones, shell and steatite. From Chāṇḍoli, comes a copper spearhead, with the tang bifurcated for hafting. The disposal of the dead presents some interesting features. Children would seem to have been exposed first and then placed in urns and buried underneath the house floor or close by. Urns or big jars were used in the case of adults who, however, were placed full length. In certain cases as many as three to five jars were used for adults; there were also adult burials without any jar. Alongside the dead were placed one or more of spouted vases and bowls, probably containing drinks and edibles. From Nevāsa comes a necklace of a child, the copper beads of which were strung with silk and cotton threads. In a similar case at Chāṅdoli, flax was used.

The Northern Deccan Chalcolithic Culture has some features not met with in the Central Indian one e.g., polished stone axes and urn-burials. The Godāvari valley received these elements through contacts with South India. In return, perhaps the Northern Deccan Chalcolithic Culture passed on to the Southern Neolithic Culture, the black-on-red pottery and copper. While further details including the early stages of this give-and-take yet remain to be worked out, it ought to be noted, as a significant fact, that the region between the Tāpti and the Upper Kṛṣṅā, was the meeting point of the cultures of the North and the South,

Carbon-14 determinations from Nevāsa and Chāṇdoli place the Northern Deccan Chalcolithic Culture in the second half of the second millennium B.C. How late and in what form the Culture continued is difficult to say at the moment. However, those who re-occupied Nevāsa later had totally given up the painted-pottery tradition. Instead, they used fiie black-and-red ware along with a scattering of the Northern Black

Polished Ware. A system, of coinage had also come into being and iron too was in use. This picture of the second settlement at Nevāsa is not dissimilar to that encountered in Central India during the early historical times.

South India

Very little is known of what followed the Microlithic Culture represented at the *teris*. However, in the later half of the third- millennium B.C., when the Harappans were dominating the North-west, we find South India occupied by people who used polished stone axes. Made of fine grained basalt, these axes had usually a splayed-out cutting-edge, pointed butt and oval section. Along with the preponderance of lithic blade tools, true microliths, probably survivals from an earlier cultural substratum were also in use. It was at a later stage that copper entered the tool-repertoire.

People preferred to live on or around granitic hills, which are a conspicuous feature of Central and Lower Deccan. Their houses were either round or rectangular, some of the recently excavated ones being 2.4-6 m. wide. The walls largely made of wattle-and-daub, were supported inside by 7½ cm. thick wooden posts and a bamboo screen. The roof was either conical or flat, made of bamboo strips and reeds and covered with dry leaves and clay.

Huge and burnt dung heaps, masses of cattle bones in their habitation debris, and paintings and bruisings of bulls on flat rock surfaces, give visible proof of what an important part cattle played in the life of these people, They were mainly pastoral people, though the occurrence of charred grains of *kulath* and boat-shaped querns in their houses indicate incipient agriculture. But in the absence of ring-stones, it is difficult to visualize how this was carried on. The other main activity of the people was felling of trees and dressing of wood, for which a large number of varied types of ground or polished tools (axes, chisels, adzes) of fine grained basalt and diorite, were made. For cutting plants and vegetables and boring holes in bone and wood, small blades, some beautifully denticulated, points and awls of chert, jasper and chalcedony, were used. Penknife-shaped blades or asymmetrical points and lunates could have been employed as teeth for harpoons and sickles. Small round balls of stone were probably used as sling stones. Extremities of cattle bones were also ground into bone tools such as chisels and spatula.

Pottery—burnished grey, buff, pale red—had highly sophisticated shapes. Besides the usual bowls and dishes, it included tea-kettle like spouted vessels for pouring liquid, strainers and cups with three or more legs and hollow pedestals. For ornaments, as elsewhere, only beads of agate, carnelian and steatite were used. Three gold ornaments have been discovered at Tekkalkota recently, proving that the local gold deposits and gold-bearing river sands were exploited.

The dead were buried in the habitation area itself. Infants, usually placed in foetal position, were buried in urns, while adults were given an extended burial in an oblong pit. With the latter, several pots were also placed, A spouted vessel in one instance and a footed cup in another, placed near the head, suggested some kind of ritual.

The more noteworthy sites- of this culture are : Brahmagiri, Sangankalla, Tekkaḷkoṭā, Piklihāl, Maski and T. Narsipur in Mysore state and Utnur and Nāgārjunikoṇḍa in Andhra Pradesh. Some of these sites have yielded, in the later phase of this culture, black-on-red ware with paintings in white on the inside. This could perhaps be ascribed to contacts with the Northern Deccan Chalcolithic or even Central Indian Chalcolithic Cultures.

The Neolithic-Chalcolithic amalgam, which seems to have been round about 2000 B.C. as Carbon-14 determination from Urnūr, in Mahbubnagar district shows, is continued up to about the middle of the first millennium B.C.; it was then overlapped by the Megalithic Culture. The latter is characterized by the use of iron swords, spears, arrow-heads and axes, black-and-red pottery and fractional burials with lithic appendage. The noteworthy burial types include cists, dolmens, dolmenoid cists, pit-burials, urn or sarcophagus-burials, 'umbrella', 'hood' and stones and menhirs, etc. While fractional burial with stone accompaniment was usual, there are instances of fractional burials without the stone component as also of full burials, extended or crouched, with or without the lithic part. On the basis of the resemblance of some shapes in the black-and-red ware from Brahmagiri with those in the black-and-red ware found at Bahal in a chalcolithic context, it is surmised that the latter might have given rise to the former. We still lack adequate data to trace, the origin, and development of the Megalithic Culture. It may, incidentally, be added that the megalithic burials find an echo in the Tamil literature of the early centuries of the Christian era.

About the beginning of the Christian era, the Megalithic Culture was overlapped by what has been called Andhra Culture on account of the occurrence of Andhra coins. The distinctive pottery of the period was a white-painted reddish-brown ware known as the Russet-coated Painted Ware. This is also the time when South India had a large volume of trade with the Roman world, as shown by the occurrence, at numerous sites, of Roman coins, glass-work, and pottery, the more noteworthy in the last item being the arretine and the amphora.

Kashmir

The valley of Kashmir has something unique to offer. Here lived, at the beginning of the 2nd millennium B.C., a people for whom underground pits were residence and bone and antlers among the principal tool materials as shown by excavations at Burzahom near Srinagar.

Cut into the *karewa* beds, the dwelling-pits were roughly circular and had a narrow mouth (1-2½ in. in diameter), tapering sides and a wide bottom (2-4½ m. in diameter). They were fairly deep (1½ to 4 m.), there being landing steps in the deeper ones. Sometimes two neighbouring pits were interconnected with a tunnelled passage. The presence of post-holes along the periphery of the mouth in certain cases suggests thatched roofing. This arrangement was dictated by extreme cold in the region.

Their tools of bone and antler comprised unilateral and bilateral harpoons, points, awls, chisels, needles and burnishers, polished stone axes, harvesters, rings and gounders. The presence of polished stone axes and the absence. of any metal from the early levels at Burzahom, make it Neolithic Culture.

In Phase II of Burzahom, the inhabitants began to use copper, though in a limited degree. Their dwellings were either of wattle-and-daub or of mud-brick. In Phase III, the structures were made of stone rubble. To this Phase belong menhirs which seem to have had a funerary association.

Belonging to Phase II and III and lying within the habitation area itself were human and animal burials. The human burials were characterized by the reclining posture of the body, use of red ochre on the bones and the trepanning of the skull. The buried animals included dog, wolf and ibex. In one instance, there were as many as five wild dogs along with antlers.

Characteristic of this culture is a burnished grey ware with mat-impressed designs on the exterior of the base. From Phase II onwards there is burnished black ware also.

How long this culture, inclusive of the metallic phase survived, is difficult to say. For, at Burzahom there is a gap between the last phase of this culture and the next occupation which, with its red-ware industry and iron implements, is ascribable to the early centuries of the Christian era.

The North-western Neolithic Culture has no parallels in India. One may have to look beyond the frontiers, perhaps towards Central Asia, for tracing the origins of the culture.

Retrospect

As time passed, elements of organized civic life became apparent: planning of the entire township; a regular drainage system; standardization of weights and measures and a system of writing came into being. Arts and crafts began to develop. By the second half of the third millennium B.C., there emerged in the north-western part of the subcontinent a civilization far more advanced than its contemporaries in other parts of the world.

But the greater part of the subcontinent was at a low level of culture, in South India, people were using microliths and polished stone axes; there were no towns not to speak of 'town-planning''. Central and Eastern India were more or less in a similar state.

By about 1700 B.C., the great Indus Civilization faded away. But it left a legacy to the regional cultures of the first quarter of the second millennium B.C. in Rājasthān and Central India.

Stone and copper or the latter alone continued to be the materials for tools throughout the 2nd millennium B.C. and it was only about the beginning of the 1st millennium B.C. that iron came on the scene. The use of iron spread fast and far and wide, and before the middle of that millennium, a full-fledged Iron Age had emerged—swords, lances, arrowheads and axes. About this time, in Northern India, the sixteen *Mahājanapadas* came into being. The capitals were fortified, and within the fortifications were located large-sized secular and religious buildings, made of kiln-burnt bricks. At Kauśāmbi, the excavators have indentified a stone-built palace. A system of coinage (punch-marked and cast copper coins) came into being. Even the common man's items, for example, pottery, show a great uniformity throughout Northern India. The Northern Black Polished Ware, while greatly concentrated in the North, has been found as far south as Chebrolu in Andhra Pradesh, as far north-west as Udegram in Afghānistān, and as far east as Candraketugarh in West Bengal. This is the time when, prior to the Christian era, the maximum cultural synthesis had been achieved in the country.

On the present evidence it is difficult to say which of the cultures has early Aryan content. It cannot be the Indus Civilization as the horse, the animal *par excellence* of the Aryans, is absent. The Indus seals do not represent it. Nor has Cemetry H Culture any strong claim as it is confined to Harappa and two sites in Bahāwalpur state, whereas the Aryan Culture was widespread. Besides, at Harappa there is a stratigraphical gap. The claim of the Copper Hoard Culture is also unsubstantiated as its typical objects, harpoon and anthropomorphic figures, have no parallels in West Asia through which the Aryans came. Nor can the Chalcolithic Culture be called Aryan, even though its pottery types— stemmed chalice and channel-spouted bowls—have their parallels in Iran through which the Aryans came, The remains of the Chalcolithic Culture should, if it is Aryan, be found in North India where the Aryans settled first. But if is not so.

The claims of the Painted Grey Ware Culture to be that of the early Aryan are supported by two facts : the region where this Culture is found—Southern Punjab, Northern Rājasthān and Uttar Pradesh—is precisely the one first occupied by the early Aryans from the Vedic to the Purāṇic times; and the accepted date-range of this culture (last quarter of 2nd millennium B.C. to 700 B.C.) is also the early Aryan period in India. Terracotta figures of the horse, as also the bones of horses found at Hastināpur tell the same story. The Mahābhārata War took place in 10th century B.C. and the Painted Grey Ware belongs to this period and is found at the sites of the war—Hastināpur, Indraprastha and Kuruksetra.

While doubt might exist about the use of iron by the *Rg-vedic* Aryans, the consensus of opinion is that by the time of the *Atharva Veda* the Aryans were fully acquainted with the metal and sharply distinguished *śyāma* or black iron from *lohita* or red copper or bronze. Of the four cultures mentioned above, the Paint Grey Ware Culture alone can claim the use of iron. From the middle of the 1st millennium B.C. to the 1st century A.D., there flourished in South India—the region where the Dravidian languages are spoken today—a Culture known as Megalithic. Tamil (Śaṅgam) literature refers to the various types of Megalithic burials. Their archaeological predecessors were the Southern Neolithic people, who by *c.* 1000 B.C. had acquired a few traits from their northerly chalcolithic neighbours. There is no inscription of the Neolithic people and the few symbols that occur on megalithic pottery are still undeciphered.

III
Fusion of Civilization

A CARDINAL FEATURE of Indian history is the influx of successive streams of peoples and cultures, all merging in the calm levels of the Indian lake. As Rabindranath Tagore observes.

"No one knows when and at whose call came pouring endless inundations of men rushing madly along to lose themselves in the sea : Aryans and non-Aryans, Dravidians and Chinese, Scythians, Huns, Pathans and Moghuls—all are mixed, merged and lost in one body."

The Indo-Pakistan subcontinent which lies along the southern fringe of the Eurasian land-mass, was one of the four great centres of culture in the ancient world, the others being Egypt, West Asia and China. Between them lay the great arid or semi-arid land-mass of Central Asia, whence nomads often sallied forth in all directions leaving fire and destruction in their wake. While other centres of civilization lay athwart great international highways which became the channels of cultural exchange, India was virtually cut off from the rest of the world by the lofty Himālayan ranges. Her isolation would have been complete if there had not been a feeder route running via Gandhāra and the Kābul valley. The main transcontinental communication connecting West Asia and China ran across the Hindu Kush and Pamirs and along the valleys of Syr-Daria and Amu-Daria and the shores of the Caspian Sea. All the routes met in Bactria. While the feeder route to India brought in invaders, the lofty mountains of India cut them off from the outside world once they had entered India, as a result of which they lost their identity in the main stream of Indian culture. The rhythms of Indian civilization have always been slower and its pulsations less violent than in West Asia. We do not have the quick and brilliant flowering of the Sumerian, Babylonian, Egyptian, Assyrian and Achaemenid art. Each, phase of cultural development tended to overlap the next, thus lending a modicum of continuity and permanence.

In India there has been a harmonious adjustment of the physical and cultural environments. Each wave of immigrants into the country was faced with three alternatives: absorption,, isolation and extinction, and the physical features within the subcontinent facilitated the coexistence of higher and lower cultures. The latter sought refuge in romote areas, uncongenial to a civilization based on agricultural economy. These refuge areas of lower cultures, which may be described as the areas of isolation or retardation, have played a vital role in the historical geography of India. They have become buffer zones separating the main foci of the regional cultures of India. The three main refuge areas are as follows :

(i) The largest single area is the Vindhyan complex, comprising the Satpura, Vindhya, Mahādeo hills; Gāwaligarh, Maikala range; Hazāribagh range, and the plateau of Chota Nāgpur, Singhbhūm and Mānbhūm.

(ii) On the west, and running at right angles to the Vindhyan complex, is the Western belt beginning with the Aravalli, and the long chain of the Western Ghats running down to the southern tip of the Peninsula.

(iii) The third system connects the great eastern forest belt; and runs parallel to the coast up to 13° N.latitude and deflects westwards to meet the Western Ghats below the plateau of Mysore.

The culture-regions of India are best defined on the basis of physical and cultural buffer zones. Bounded by the Arāvalli and the desert of Rājasthān in the east and the Sulaimān and Kirthar ranges in the west, is the Indus basin, draining the Central Himālayas. This can be divided at the point where the desert and the hills converge near the Bugti country, giving rise to the Punjab and Sind. The Ganga basin begins from the Indo-Gaṅgā divide and extends eastwards. Its delta forms the deltaic Bengal. The valley of the Brahmaputra constitutes Assam. The triangular area forming the southern flanks of the Gaṅgā basin, drained by the rivers Chambal, Banās, Śiprā, Śoṇa and Narmadā (linking Central India with the Arabian Sea), is Mālwa and its eastern appendage, Bundelkhand. Lying south of the Vindhya range and constituting the upper basin of the rivers Godāvari and Kṛṣṇā, is Mahārāshtra. The lower basins of these two major rivers constitute Āndhra. The rocky triangle formed by the Eastern and the Western Ghāts and comprising the southern basin of the Kṛśṇa is Mysore or Karṇāṭaka. The southern littoral from 13"

N.latitude, and beginning from the construction of the Nagari hills and the Pulicat lake, is Tamilnād. The small coastal plain, on either side of the Pālghāt gap in the Western Ghāts, is Kerala, The valley of the Mahānadi is Orissa. The northern part of the western littoral and the peninsula of Saurāshtra constitute Gujarāt. The semi-arid area to the north of Gujarāt, occupying either side of the Arāvalli, constitutes Rājasthān.

The communication system is regulated by physical features. One line of communication runs from the openings in the north-west, across the upper courses of the Sindhu and its tributaries and along the Ganga to its delta. The second ancient highway (now called the Great Deccan Road) runs from the Central Gaṇgā basin (ancient Magadha) to the West Coast along and across the Vindhyas. The third highway links the West Coast with the East Coast and skirts the Godāvari and Kṛṣṅa. Lastly, the Tamilnād is connected to Andhra Pradesh and Karṇāṭaka by the Nallamalai hills. These four highways constitute the four arms of what is called the "Z" pattern. This pattern, so well demonstrated by Indian history and archaeology, isolates regions like Assam, Kashmir, Gujarāt, and Orissa. In these areas of relative isolation occurs a curious pattern of survivals and cultural development. Gujarāt is an instance of the area of relative isolation. It received maritime influences first and continental influences later. Thus the Indus Civilization with its maritime character survived in a pure form in Saurashtra for a longer period than in the rest of India.

The physical features of the subcontinent and the communication system conditioned by them help us to understand the cultural diversity within the subcontinent. The main river basins constitute the areas of attraction, and the tribal areas are those of retardation and isolation. Between them lay the areas of relative isolation.

Such is the geographical framework in which the great synthesis has been taking place throughout Indian history. Various peoples and cultures that moved into this subcontinent were subjected to the dynamic factors imposed by her geography, primarily in her relation with the rest of Eurasia and secondarily also within the country. There was access by land from the west (Khyber and Bolan passes) and from the east and north-east (Burma and Tibet). The other main line is maritime. Taking the fundamental concept of areas of attraction, relative isolation, and isolation, primarily based on geography, we can define the pattern of development of civilization in India as the horizontal expansion of the higher cultures, leading to a contraction and isolation of the lower cultures in different parts of the country, at different periods and at different cultural levels.

From the close of the Second Ice Age in the Punjab and Kashmir and its corresponding phase in the Peninsula, India seems to have had during the Early Stone Age two stone tool-making traditions. So far no remains of the men who made those tools have been found. It is therefore difficult to say whether these different traditions belong to distinct racial groups or the same racial stock. If there were two separate racial groups, the subsequent development within the Early Stone Age would represent some kind of fusion, either of the tool traditions only or of the two racial groups as well.

The next stage in man's development the Middle Stone Age, poses similar ptoblems. The tools are different in type and raw material from those of the Early Stone Age. But the basic techniques remain the same. Although there are no skeletal remains of the Middle Stone Age Culture, it might be taken to represent new immigrants under whose impact the old culture changed.

The last phase of the food-collecting stage, which we have designated as Late Stone Age, was in many ways more advanced than, the two earlier stages. Beginnings of agriculture and domestication of animals might have taken place during this time or towards its close. The distribution of the remains of this Stone Age shows that at one time the entire Indo-Pakistan subcontinent, or large parts of it, were occupied by these food-gatherers. Later, the expansion of the food-producers pushed them into hilly and forested areas. Some scholars think that the primitive tribes in India like the Kādats of Cochin and the Cencus of the Godāvari basin are residual elements of this cultural stage.

In view of the general typological affinity of the microlithic industries of the Indo-Pākistān subcontinent, the basic similarity of its environments with those of Africa, West Asia, Ceylon and Australia, the admitted earlier existence of such cultures in these countries and the suspected Veddid strain {Australoid) in some of the present tribes and the skeletal material from a few sites like Lānghnaj and Nevāsa, would seem to show that even this Stone Age Culture is in some way indebted to the influence of the adjoining regions.

It is now known where and how in India the transition to a higher way of life took place—a life marked by permanent settlements, ground or polished tools, domestication of animals, the beginnings of agriculture, and the first use of copper tools. Surveys have brought to light several areas, each with some special features : painted pottery of a red fabric in the north-west and west, and, then of a grey fabric also painted ; preponderance of polished tools from Central Deccan up to Salem district of Tamilnādu, and on the flanks of the Vindhya range in Madhya Pradesh and along the Kaimur hills of Uttar Pradesh. In Assam and Orissa, these polished stone tools are of a different character (square shouldered).

The considerable regional differentiation is partly due to the availability of raw material and nearness to continental highways, and partly to the arrival of new peoples or new ideas. The Indus Civilization is essentially "Indian" in character. Several European scholars, however, argue that its painted pottery tradition might have been initially derived from Irān, while the idea of town planning might have come from Irāq, both preceded by the advent of food-production in the submontane zone of Irāq. We have here an excellent synthesis of the West Asian and Indian (Indus) venture in urbanization.

Within India itself, the early food-producing communities on the Narmadā, Chambal and Banās, Godāvari, Pravara, Tāpti and Girna seem to represent a distant echo of the movements of peoples and ideas, again from Irān and West Asia. Two items of these cultures, pottery types and their decorative motifs, and cereals like lentil and linseed point to West Asian origins. Penetration of West Asian influences, by whatever cultural and racial names we might call them, is postulated for the Central Deccan Neolithic, though some scholars would connect one of its chief elements, the ground or polished stone axe, with South East Asia. There is little doubt that South East Asian contacts were responsible for the introduction of the square shouldered axe in Orissa and Assam, This may be roughly assigned to the first millennium B.C.

Towards the end of this period another large movement of peoples bearing the Painted Grey Ware is evident in the Gaṅgā-Yamunā Doab, the Punjab and the Sarasvati valley in Rājasthān. The juxtaposition of several Painted Grey Ware sites with many of the towns and villages mentioned in connection with the Kaurava-Pāṇḍava story in the *Mahābhārata* is cited to show that in all probability the bearers of this pottery were a branch of the Aryans, who are believed to have entered India a few centuries earlier.

If so, the ochre-coloured pottery which is now found in still earlier deposits from Chandigarh in the north to Vāranāsi in the east and at one or two sites where previously copper hoards had been found, should belong to a still earlier branch of the Aryans or some pre-Aryan people. Likewise, we shall have to attribute a fine black-and-red pottery, occasionally painted in white on the inside and found at a number of sites in the ancient Magadha and Kosala to some Aryan or pre-Aryan tribes, spreading eastwards from Eastern Rājasthān.

Whether we call it a fusion or synthesis, there is little doubt that it is the authors of some of the above mentioned cultures (strictly speaking, pottery industries) who later get a habitation and a name in the Vedic literature, Purāṇas and early Jaina and Buddhist texts.

But a common, generalized pattern of material as well as linguistic culture which brought about the Mauryan empire in the North and the Āndhra empire in the Deccan effacing various regional or local manifestations is now documented by archaeology in particular by the spread of iron all over India, and certain types of pottery fabrics, beads and other items of material culture. The same process further south seems to have started a few centuries earlier, as the distribution, of the megalithic monuments and the Dravidian languages show.

Further fusion of cultures look place with the spread of Sanskrit or when Sanskrit became a court language both in the North and the South. With that were adopted, with great modifications at times, Brahmanic gods and goddesses and a variety of practices which are best described in the Tamil classic *Śilappadikāram.*

Archaeological and linguistic evidence points to the evolution of Pan-Indian culture, Behind this is the main agency of this fusion—the man himself. The geographic isolation of this subcontinent and its distinct personality have led to the emergence of an ethnic conglomerate which may be described as "Indian". According to the latest system of classification, India can at best be conceived as having a single race with varying substocks or at best two races. The synthesis is the result of millennia of conflict and interaction of the various groups of people who migrated into this country. This struggle and the consequent instability of racial conditions can be ascribed to the physical diversity and the favourable geographic factors resulting from the areas of retardation and isolation of cultures. Thus the earlier elements that could not get adapted to the new culture and technology protected themselves by retreating to the forests and hilly areas. This struggle was economic and also social. Socio- anthropologists have shown that the aboriginal tribes in India represent the residual substrata or a "primitive isolate" in their transformation to a peasant and higher culture. The question whether all these are autochthonous or only the Australoid group as such and the rest due to migrations from the East and West is not yet answered,

Several attempts have been made to isolate the contribution of each of these elements without any convincing evidence. For example Negrito elements are supposed to have given us the worship of the *pipal (Ficus religiosa),* while the emergence of Kṛṣṇa as the supreme god symbolizes the synthesis of several non-Aryan and Aryan concepts and practices.

A study of the existing main language groups, viz.,. Sanskrit (Indo-Aryan) ; Tibeto-Burman ; Ausrro-Asian; Dravidian and their geographical distribution shows that considerable admixture has taken place between these groups. Today it is not possible to trace back all the original elements from each of these language groups, However, studies of Jules Bloch, Burrow, Chatterji, Przyluski, Sylvain Levi and Schmidt, and lately by Tolstoy indicate that though Sanskrit and its offshoots—the regional languages—now dominate most of Northern India, examples can be cited of borrowings by Sanskrit from the other three groups. This fact together with the present distribution of these languages is suggestive of the original spread of the languages within India and the great fission that has taken place in course of the millennia. Non-Aryan and pre-Aryan words, phrases and even sentence patterns have been adopted by Sanskrit and made its own.

Racial and cultural synthesis is also reflected in our myths and legends narrated in the Purānas and other literature. A comparative study of the early and late Vedic literature points to their advance first eastward into Magadha, from the Gaṅgā-Yamunā Doab and then southwards. This conquest was not only geographical but also cultural. Yet it was not a one way traffic. When Bihār and parts of West Bengal were being Aryanized, the Aryans absorbed some of the local culture (myths and practices). This is well illustrated by the story of the Vena and the Niṣādas; the recognition of *anuloma* and *pratiloma* marriages by thp Dharma Śāstras ; the Puranic division of the human race (in three main stocks, Manavas, Ailas and Sudyumna and the tracing of fictitious genealogies by such distant dynasties as Colas and Pāṇḍvas from Manu through Turvasas. Indianization of extra-Indian myths had started much earlier and is documented in archaeology by the Indus seal where a Gilgamash-like hero stands between two tigers instead of lions as in Sumer, and in literature by the Flood legend,

Horizontal expansion of the Aryans in space, as also mention of the non-Aryans and miscegenration of myths singly and cumultatively, illustrate the continuous process of cultural fusion and synthesis.

This synthesis did not stop with the dawn of the historical period. It is a continuous process like the ever flowing Gaṅgā. Right at the beginning came the Persians, then the Greeks and later the Śakas, Kuṣānas, Hūṇas and Gurjaras. Archaeology— monuments and inscriptions of the first thousand years (500 B.C.— A.D. 500) bears enough testimony to the impact of these newer people, from the west and Central Asia, Hardly had the fusion and synthesis of these peoples been completed when the others came, first the Arabs, then the Turks, Afghāns and Mongols. This gave us the fine flowering of Indian Culture under the Mughals. Its decline ushered in the Europeans from the West ; and they gave birth to the Indo-Anglian Culture. But this is not all. Within India, the partition uprooted millions in the east and west and the fresh arrival of Panjābis, Sindhis and Bengalis and of Tibetans in a different context, has set in motion a new cultural synthesis.